seeds planted in concrete

bianca sparacino

Copyright © 2015 by Bianca Sparacino. All rights reserved. Published by
Thought Catalog Books, a publishing house in Williamsburg, Brooklyn run by
The Thought & Expression Company (www.thought.is). Art and book
production directed by Chris Lavergne with the assistance of Natalie Shields,
Mink Choi, Mark Kupasrimonkol, Ruby June, and KJ Parish.

For those who loved me like a
soft dawn

For those who loved me like a
hurricane

i.

You will hurt people.
You will hurt, and you will be hurt.
However, you will also love, and you
will be loved in the most magnificent
ways. To live life is to understand that
together these extremes thrive within
us — our heart is both a blessing and a
blade. To put our soul into the hands of
someone who could wound it or heal it
is quite possibly the most courageously
beautiful risk we take. It is like looking
someone right in the eye and saying
"You may hurt me, but you may also
love me, and I am willing to take that
chance. I am willing to trust."

ii.

to hurt

iii.

to feel

iv.

When rain taps against your window like an
eager child, it is important to remember
that even the world cries—even the sky, which
holds everything together, falls a part from time
to time.

When you
are not
your best,
I will
be your
best.

v.

The oxygen at the summit of Mount Everest is the same oxygen that has been delicately knit within your lungs; the elements at the bottom of the ocean are dotted like wildflowers along the surface of your skin. Let this reassure you—at the highest and lowest points of life, you were made to endure. You were made to survive.

When you are not your best, I will be your best.

vi.

Sometimes I forget that we are all just living
between the lines of life — between the aches
and the joys, between what is happy and what is
sad within us. Sometimes I forget that I am not
alone in that, for no one lives in either extreme
— in perpetual bliss or perpetual sorrow. We are
all just playing with darkness and light, we are
all just trying to find our harmony.

vii.

You inspired me.

For that, you were worth every inch of love I
had to give; you were worth the fall, the bruised
knees. For that, I kissed the weapon that was
your warm mouth with a soft tongue and I
endured. I waited.

viii.

Sometimes people don't understand why we love the way we love, why we stay the way we stay. Sometimes people cannot comprehend that at times we do not love because we want to, but rather, we love because we have someone else's blood within our veins, we have someone else's hands clenched tightly around our heart.

ix.

I held you in the dips of my paper arms and
whispered, "don't feel blue. You're not the only
one with holes in you. Look closely—parts of me
are weathered too."

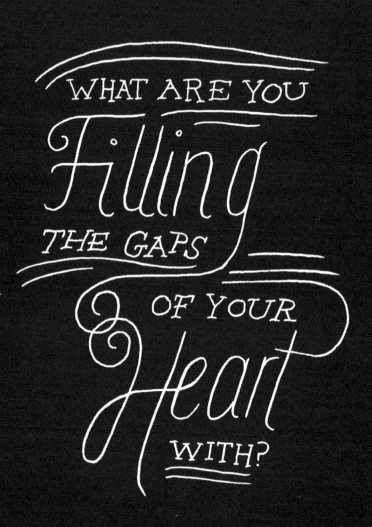

WHAT ARE YOU Filling THE GAPS OF YOUR Heart WITH?

x.

What a tragedy it is to tell yourself not to be afraid. It's like telling yourself not to be sad, not to be happy, not to experience some of your most visceral and native human instincts. The truth is that every individual is afraid, every soul gets scared, every heart gets hesitant, but that is not to be sanitized, that is not to be dismissed. Feel your fear, but do not let it be a barrier, let it be a break—a small crack where you prove to yourself that you are strong in spite of it, a reminder that you can leap even if your legs are trembling.

xi.

Do not ruin yourself with hollow longing.
Your body is a sanctuary, a place where love
and grief flow like crashing rapids against
your spine. Its time to take your hands off of
your thighs, and your gaze off of the marks
that adorn your hips like ornaments.

The universe gave up celestial pieces of
itself to sculpt you.
It is time to honor that.

xii.

There may come a day when they fall out of love with you. Do not let this be the day you fall out of love with you. How long they choose to stay will never be your decision, but how you choose to rise is.

<u>xiii.</u>

On the days in which you look at your palms and
you see weeds, promise me that you will tell
yourself that they are worthy of gardens—
promise me that you will remember just how
many hands they have held, just how many
hearts they have touched.

xiv.

The truth of it all is that you may not know
what you deserve right this moment, and
that is okay. You will grow to figure it out.
Until then, just promise me that you will
believe with merciless conviction, with
ruthless certainty, that you do not deserve
to be unhappy. Promise me you will believe
that you mean something.

with you
by my side

Love,

everything
Screams
life.

xv.

Do not hide your wounds—for even flowers
bloom within concrete fractures and damaged
fragments make up the most intricate mosaics.
Promise me that you will never conceal your
cracks, for I will only ever see them as places in
which to fill with love.

With you by my side love, everything screams
life.

xvi.

I never believed in ghosts until you left, for
I could not see you, but I could still feel
you. No, I never believed in ghosts until I
loved one.

xvii.

I've sent my heart to war for you so many times,
yet never has it said, "this is too much."
Never has it backed down.

We are constantly reminded of how trivial
we are, how fragile and negligible our goose
bumps seem compared to the magic of the
bangs and whispers of the universe when it
collides within itself. Like a jaded generation we
have been taught to write ourselves off, to
commit our shallow meanings to losing and
finding ourselves alone, to shutting down and
shutting out bitter hearts while staying awake in
the depth of the night just trying to hold on to
moments of smaller magic. I am standing in a
place where I can see the turn of the world and I
am not afraid because I am reminded of the
enchantment and the passion we shared, the
ruthless dedication we made to devouring each
other whole.

Don't fall in love. That was the one rule I gave to
myself, etching my name into a vessel of contra-
dictions that described the kind of girl who
fashioned papier-mâché wings out of historical
let downs while roping herself to the limbs of an
idea in order to stay stable. It was the coldest of
winters when I broke that rule. The spring had
left a hollow shell of empty promises that I rolled
into my sheets and wrapped myself in whenever
I felt like feeling. It was then that you came to
me, gathering your breath within my ribcage in
order to keep my core warm, you laced your
beauty between my palms and wove me my own
hope. You were tender and unguarded and I knew
that you wouldn't know the brutality of broken
things even though you loved one.

I am in awe of everything you refused to give up on. We had passion and opportunity and I almost convinced myself that we were the winners in the war of winter. I held you like nostalgia in the middle of my mind, taking a moment to flutter my eyelashes over the heat of your skin, immortalizing you in my memory before I plucked away at your faultlessness like flower petals at midnight.

Just know that you discovered me. We were so close, but like the ghosts of my past I felt you at my throat the minute you questioned the hesitance of my heartbeat. I'm writing this to say I'm sorry. I'm poison the way I love, so this is my confession.

This is a blueprint to the mysteries I tucked into my pores whenever our matchstick frames came together. This is the goodbye you never got.

do you remember
The Day
Love Broke
down the walls
Within Your Chest?

xix.

Those who insist that you cannot exist in two
places at once have never left their heart in the
hands of someone who lives across an ocean.

XX.

You are not a lonely interlude,
In the song of someone's life.
Do you remember the day love broke down the
walls within your chest?

xxi.

One day you will meet someone who crashes
into your bones like a wildfire, setting your
heart ablaze, and together you will burn and
spark and love until you wake up one morning
beside the ashes of what was. However, it won't
end there—for just as wood still holds an ember
long after a blaze, you will always taste forest
fires in the back of your throat whenever you
hear their name.

xxii.

Love, like a weathered star, does not disappear
when it has met its dying day. Instead, it swells
within its boundary, it surges and it builds until
it is simply too painful, too vast, to ever be
contained within a human heart. No, love never
leaves. It ruptures within you, like a thousand
year old sun, like an ancient constellation,
leaving parts of itself scattered across your
ribcage, leaving memories tucked beneath
your skin.

you wake up

Every

Single day

with the opportunity

To start feeling
again.

xxiii.

The human heart has only 4 chambers. So tell
me—if we fill it with fear, with hatred, with
doubt and with reservation, where will we grow
our love?

xxiv.

As children we were taught not to play with fire,
so we closed ourselves off and kept ourselves
safe, forgetting about the flame within our
hearts—forgetting about the spark within
our souls.

XXV.

Free creature, be soft again, for your voice
has hardened and the Earth has made you stiff.
Tell me, have your limbs forgotten your lover's
essence? Has your heart forgotten the poetry
you become when you are stirred? Do you not
remember how your mother kissed a sunrise
into your cheek every morning, for that light is
still trapped within your skin, and you are soft
there. Do not fashion yourself in the image of
restraint or tarnished steel, do not turn to brick
in the midst of uncertainty. May the wild bird
within your heart fly, and may you dip your
wings in ink so that your words fall from the
sky, staining the Earth with love.

xxvi.

On the days you feel like you have no music left
inside your dry bones, remember that your
heartbeat is too a song—and it is quite possibly
the truest, most beautiful soundtrack to
your life.

xxvii.

Listen—

You are not a lonesome freeway with a history
of accidents, or the damaged record of every
pair of palms that tried to unravel you. You are
not a regret, not a letdown. Here you are, living
like a scarlet war—no part of you wants to be
real. This is when you need to open like a bud to
the arms that hold you; this is when you need to
let them love you, even if you'd prefer to run
from the sun into the shadowy sirens that call
your name like a prayer.

Repeat after me—you are a vessel of roses, and
you wont always be in bloom, but I promise that
the frost never stays for long. I promise that the
light will find you.

Focus
less on
being
beautiful,
and more on
being **REAL.**

xxviii.

to love

xxix.

to heal

<u>xxx.</u>

To the moon,
Who loves so selflessly,
That it wakes up to darkness every night
For the waves that rely on its pull
And the mad dreamers who rely on its light

xxxi.

Somewhere, tucked away in the vastness of it
all, hidden between the horizon and the sea,
there exists a world where you are loving the
one that got away, where the words you never
allowed yourself to say flow freely between
your teeth. There exists a realm where you did
things differently—where you chose the other
path. Maybe you are happier there, though that
is not the point, for maybe you aren't. Maybe,
just maybe, despite circumstance, despite
regret, you are exactly where you need to be.
The only thing stopping you from realizing that
is the way you whisper "what if."

<u>xxxii.</u>

Imagine how different the world would be if
from the rooftops of our very own apartments, if
from the crowd filled city streets, we yelled our
love for one another rather than our hate.
Always remember that the human heart is
approximately the size of two hands clasped
together. There is no coincidence in that.

Take your life back from your flaws. You are so much more than your mistakes, and the things you dislike about yourself. Tell me, who were you before you let your flaws define you? Before you zoned in on your shortcomings, your imperfections and your weaknesses? Who were you before you allowed such things to dictate your existence? Before you started saying no to living when it tapped on your shoulder because you were disappointed with your body, because you didn't believe in yourself, because you constantly compared your value to what others portrayed around you? Who were you before you let your faults limit you, and what have you given up, what opportunities have you held like sand between your fingertips because you empowered your insecurities instead of empowering your confidence?

Take your life back from what broke you. The past is meant to etch lessons into our bones, yet we huddle ourselves within the warmth of its familiarity, we cradle our bodies within its weighted grips because we allow for what broke us to build us. Promise me that you will never again run back to what cracked you, what fractured your heart, your mind, your soul. Promise me that you will no longer hand yourself over to the man or the woman who loved you like poison, that you will no longer give life to the experiences that haunt you like ghosts. Promise me that you will find what it is that will grow within you like wildfire and plant it within the depths of your scars. You will mend. Allow yourself to.

Take your life back from your flatline. It is a tragedy to think that we often allow for an increase in our heartbeats to deter us from new experiences. We think that the resounding pound chiming throughout our chests when we are challenged is something we should protect ourselves from, something that is a sign of danger. Trust me when I say that the quickening of your pulse, the thud of your heart against your ribcage—that is the most carnally beautiful reminder that you are alive. Use your heart like a compass; let it be a prompt for curiosity, rather than fear. Stop silencing your guideline, because when you run from what enlivens you, when you play small in a world that is begging you to play big, you sell yourself short. You cheat yourself of the potential you hold, you cheat the world of your unique contribution, and you stay unsatisfied. You stay stagnant. Get a little scared from time to time, take your life back from the baseline.

At the end of the day, you are ultimately the curator of your life. So, when you wake up each morning—take your life back. Take your life back from anything that feeds negativity within it, take your life back from the things that do not grow you, or move you. Make a pact with yourself to simply take control of who you will have the ability to be, and what you will have the ability to do, when you start to harness for yourself all of the energy you used to put into nourishing a life that never felt like it was truly yours. Take your life back and grow it into something that inspires you to rise with conviction and passion. Take your life back and grow it into something that you are proud of.

xxxiv.

"Nothing truly beautiful ever asks for attention."
This quote has stuck with me ever since I heard
my coworker speak the words. Nothing truly
beautiful ever asks for attention—it just naturally
exists, as it is, in confidence and boldness.

Remember this the next time you chase some-
one you think you love. Remember this the next
time you feel as if you need to compete for the
attention of someone you admire. Generationally
speaking, we often feel the need to prove
ourselves to the heart we regard. We often feel
the need to change ourselves to better suit their
needs, we often wonder if we are exactly what
they are looking for, or if they have other options.
I have heard the sentiment many times over, I
have seen it dissect beautiful moments and
sensationalize less than beautiful relationships.
Stop the "If onlys" and the "But maybes." Trust
me when I say that those do not exist within the
boundaries of the love you want. They only exist
within the reality of the love you chase.

The most awe-inspiring person I ever had the
privilege of loving planted his feet firmly in front
of me and said "This is what I want." There was
courage, transparency. There was declaration.

There was no insecurity, there was no need to
compare myself to others or compete. The most
awe-inspiring person I ever had the privilege of
loving chose me every single day, and I chose
him. When that wasn't the case, we parted ways.
We didn't drag it out, we didn't try to convince

the other. We didn't feel the need to grip, and chase something that did not fulfill us or inspire us. It was natural, and organic, and it allowed for me to feel deeply and confidently. That is the kind of love you want.

Do not chase another human being. Instead, chase your curiosity. Chase your development and your goals. Chase your passion. Strive to work for something bigger than yourself, and instead of trying to convince someone that you fit within their world, strive to build your own. Relationships are not melting pots. They are unions. You walk into them with your own visions, your own hunger, and when you are confident in that, when you allow for that to thrive within you, you never break yourself down to appease the pursuit. You simply exist, as you are, and when you meet someone who does as well, when you meet someone who chooses you within that, you thrive together, and that creates a dynamic that is ever growing and influential.

Nothing beautiful ever asks for attention. Let that be a testament. The truly carnal relation-ship, the attraction, the pull to another human being—it simply survives. It flourishes. It is the kind of beauty that lives within ribcages, that surges throughout bones, that you cannot explain, that allows you to "just know." It is never bred from contest; it is never bred from uncer-tainty. You will never have to work to inspire it within someone, because it will simply exist within them.

Understand that life is not a straight line. Life is not a set timeline of milestones. It is okay if you don't finish school, get married, find a job that supports you, have a family, make money, and live comfortably all by this age, or that age. It's okay if you do, as long as you understand that if you're not married by 25, or a Vice President by 30—or even happy, for that matter—the world isn't going to condemn you. You are allowed to backtrack. You are allowed to figure out what inspires you. You are allowed time, and I think we often forget that. We choose a program right out of high school because the proper thing to do is to go straight to University. We choose a job right out of University, even if we didn't love our program, because we just invested time into it. We go to that job every morning because we feel the need to support ourselves abundantly. We take the next step, and the next step, and the next step, thinking that we are fulfilling some checklist for life, and one day we wake up depressed. We wake up stressed out. We feel pressured and don't know why. That is how you ruin your life.

You ruin your life by choosing the wrong person. What is it with our need to fast-track relation-ships? Why are we so enamored with the idea of first becoming somebody's rather than some-bodies? Trust me when I say that a love bred out of convenience, a love that blossoms from the need to sleep beside someone, a love that caters to our need for attention rather than passion, is a love that will not inspire you at 6am when you

we loved like BEASTS and parted like glaciers.

roll over and embrace it. Strive to discover foundational love, the kind of relationship that motivates you to be a better man or woman, the kind of intimacy that is rare rather than right there. "But I don't want to be alone," we often exclaim. Be alone. Eat alone, take yourself on dates, sleep alone. In the midst of this you will learn about yourself. You will grow, you will figure out what inspires you, you will curate your own dreams, your own beliefs, your own stunning clarity, and when you do meet the person who makes your cells dance, you will be sure of it, because you are sure of yourself. Wait for it. Please, I urge you to wait for it, to fight for it, to make an effort for it if you have already found it, because it is the most beautiful thing your heart will experience.

You ruin your life by letting your past govern it. It is common for certain things in life to happen to you. There will be heartbreak, confusion, days where you feel like you aren't special or purposeful. There are moments that will stay with you, words that will stick. You cannot let these define you—they were simply moments, they were simply words. If you allow for every negative event in your life to outline how you view yourself, you will view the world around you negatively. You will miss out on opportunities because you didn't get that promotion five years ago, convincing yourself that you were stupid. You will miss out on affection because you assumed your past love left you because you weren't good enough, and now you don't believe the man or the woman who urges you to believe you are. This is a cyclic, self-fulfilling prophecy.

If you don't allow yourself to move past what happened, what was said, what was felt, you will look at your future with that lens, and nothing will be able to breach that judgment. You will keep on justifying, reliving, and fueling a perception that shouldn't have existed in the first place.

You ruin your life when you compare yourself to others. The amount of Instagram followers you have does not decrease or increase your value. The amount of money in your bank account will not influence your compassion, your intelligence, or your happiness. The person who has two times more possessions than you does not have double the bliss, or double the merit. We get caught up in what our friends are liking, who our significant others are following, and at the end of the day this not only ruins our lives, but it also ruins us. It creates within us this need to feel important, and in many cases we often put others down to achieve that.

You ruin your life by desensitizing yourself. We are all afraid to say too much, to feel too deeply, to let people know what they mean to us. Caring is not synonymous with crazy. Expressing to someone how special they are to you will make you vulnerable. There is no denying that. However, that is nothing to be ashamed of. There is something breathtakingly beautiful in the moments of smaller magic that occur when you strip down and are honest with those who are important to you. Let that girl know that she inspires you. Tell your mother you love her in front of your friends.

Express, express, express. Open yourself up, do not harden yourself to the world, and be bold in who, and how, you love. There is courage in that.

You ruin your life by tolerating it. At the end of the day you should be excited to be alive. When you settle for anything less than what you innately desire, you destroy the possibility that lives inside of you, and in that way you cheat both yourself and the world of your potential. The next Michelangelo could be sitting behind a Macbook right now writing an invoice for paperclips, because it pays the bills, or because it is comfortable, or because he can tolerate it. Do not let this happen to you. Do not ruin your life this way. Life and work, and life and love, are not irrespective of each other. They are intrinsically linked. We have to strive to do extraordinary work, we have to strive to find extraordinary love. Only then will we tap into an extraordinarily blissful life.

xxxvi.

I want to lend you my eyes so that you can
finally see just how spectacular you are in the
reflection of the nameless, and newfangled
colours that dance within my vision when I
see you.

I want to
inspire
within you
a feverish
unapologetic
thirst for life.

xxxvii.

Love is bred from the Earth within your soul,
and if you faithfully expose the soil within your
heart to the elements of life, if you mercilessly
dedicate yourself to cultivating and growing its
territory—despite the famines it has endured in
the past - you will wake up one morning, and
turn your head to see the most beautiful
harvest, sleeping beside you.

xxxviii.

Despite only accounting for four percent of the universe, the planets and the stars, the galaxies and the nebulae, are the most breathtakingly beautiful aspects of creation. The next time you feel small within your doubt, within your flaws, within your darkness, remember that you still have constellations within you. Your strengths, your attributes, your unwavering compassion, the way you care so deeply—that is what people notice when they see you, and that is what makes you a phenomenon.

<u>xxxix.</u>

Frisson is the swell within your cells that occurs when you listen to a passage of music that deeply moves you.

When I told you that you were a symphony playing throughout my bones, you laughed and said that people couldn't be songs. If only you knew... You are the greatest piece of music I have ever crashed into. You are the overture within my heartbeat.

You, my dear—
I could listen to you for days.

xl.

Do not fret if you have yet to find it, this lucid
and dreamlike love they speak of, this fervent
and inspiring tenderness. Do not fret if you have
yet to find it, rather, open your heart to an atlas
and stretch your fingertips towards the sky—for
the world is also capable of holding your hand,
and my god, is it ever beautiful, the kind of love
you find tucked away within yourself when the
Earth opens your eyes.

xli.

The law of conservation states that energy
cannot be destroyed or abolished. Instead,
it manifests within new forms.

Therefore, you have not lost in love; you
have not been robbed of your treasured muse,
or your cherished connection. Your passion has
not died, and the fire within your ribcage has
not turned to ash. You have not lost, for the
energy that roped itself within each and every
lover, within each and every conversation and
idea, is being gifted to you in renewed ways. The
beauty of a sunset, the smile from a stranger on
a disheartening day, the stillness of your
surroundings when you stop in the middle of
the street because you feel something
exquisitely familiar was over you.

This energy, it will move through you
like a thread, but you must not get attached to
its concreteness. You must give it back to the
world in which gifted it to you. You must set it
free, and it will come back in the form of a
second chance, or a moment of inspiring beauty
shared in passing with the Earth.

No, you have not lost. You are
surrounded by him, by her, by your memories,
your destinies, your life in new form.

IF WE CLOSE OURSELVES Off HOW WILL THE Light GET IN?

xlii.

I do not hate you for the things you did to kill
your sadness. For the mouths you kissed,
thinking of the life they would breathe into your
hollowness, for the opportunities you missed
because you felt worthless. I do not hate you for
being confused, for running before you knew
how to calm the shadows that danced inside
of you.

Trust me when I say that I will love you in your
humanness. I will love you for your twists, I will
love you for your faults. Trust me when I say
that I will love it all.

xliii.

Isn't it beautiful? How our hearts can
effortlessly fall in love with something as simple
as a smile. How one single spark can inspire
wildfires within us, and how the idea of
forgetting the way someone made us feel is just
as absurd as the coast forgetting the ocean, or
the Earth forgetting the sun. Isn't it beautiful?
How ruthlessly we still hope, how deeply we
still surrender.

xliv.

I was a shade of scarlet,
he was a shade of yellow,
and all I wanted to do was live life
in a perfect shade of orange,
like the exceptional merging of colours,
the unique communion of hues
that dances within each sunset.

We Seek
CONNECTION,
yet We
Avoid
Eye contact.

xlv.

We live our whole lives convincing ourselves
that a racing heart is a sign of endangerment,
when it is quite simply the most carnal and
organic way our body shows us that we are still
alive. Don't be afraid of your beating heart. It is
the very animation of vitality, and the very
representation of the strength you harness
within you. Embrace it. Seek out situations that
stir it. Challenge it. Use it as your compass, for
there is nothing more beautiful than the quiet
thud of ruthless passion against a shaking
ribcage.

xlvi.

The human body is comprised of 11 concrete elements, but at the end of the day, it is simply the elements of hope, and love, that make us truly real.

xlvii.

You exist solely, as a beat within my heart,
and in this way,
I keep you alive,
while you keep me alive.

xlviii.

I will meet you within the holes of the sky, the untouched tunnels where dreamers stamp out the supernovas. I will meet you within the intensity of the sea, between the waves and the horizon—that small sliver of Earth where feeling is preserved like a mounted butterfly in a glass case. Where is the paradise that surges beyond love?

I will meet you there.

<u>xlix.</u>

The human eye has three ways of deciphering
colour. The Mantis Shrimp, on the other hand,
has sixteen, allowing it to see rainbows of over
sixty hues. Trust me when I say that there is so
much more out there. There are so many more
colours to grasp, so many more ways to love, so
many more things to feel—things that exist
outside of human certainty, beauty that thrives
outside of boundary and formula. Allow yourself
to see it all, and if you cannot, allow yourself to
believe in it indefinitely until you do.

REMEMBER–

IF IT IS NOT

LOVE OR PASSION,

IT IS POISON.

I.

You yourself are made up of atoms that rained down on to Earth billions of years ago. So when you meet someone and you swear that you have known them before, that you have felt them before, know that there is no coincidence in that finally your cells are reunited, and at last, it feels like you are home.

li.

If every form of nature looked the same we
wouldn't marvel in its beauty. If every
mountain overlooked a parallel scene, if every
flower bloomed in uninspired ways, the Earth
would not steal us of our breath. Use this as a
lesson. Your eyes, your hands, your marvelous
smile—those are all your unique contribution
to the matchless beauty of nature. You are a
stunning rarity; you don't need to be fixed.

lii.

Scientists insist that our bodies are made up of
seventy percent water. Let this fact remind you
of how wild you are. Whenever a drop of sweat
falls from your brow, or whenever something
stirs within you the emotion that spearheads
a tear, you are being turned inside out, as if the
very salt of the Earth is trying to reunite with
the external world in search of the rousing
depths of the ocean that crafted it.

Foolish is the man who does not trust his
wild. No amount of rationale will stop the
cosmos from taking back what they bore in you.
There will come a night when the very stars
smell of your perfume. There will come a time
when the very trees you walk by in your daily
routine reflect the same colour green you
admire in your lovers eyes; for we were born
from the Earth, and one day, we will return to it.

liii.

Soon the day came, when I realized that I did
not need to find you—for you were already
within me, like blood in my veins.

INSTEAD OF CHOOSING
— TO MERELY —
EXIST,
I URGE YOU TO
EXPERIENCE
LIFE
I URGE YOU TO LIVE.

liv.

The rare union of love and absolute freedom—
the ability to look at him, at her, with a curious,
liberated heart, and see the world differently
every single time.

lv.

To say, "I love you" is to choose,
is to endure,
is to meet a person's twists
and have no desire to untie them.

lvi.

Whenever you feel like your uniqueness is a
downfall, remember that of great poetry and
art—the masterpieces are always misunderstood,
the hallmarks are always matchless.

You are a Mona Lisa smile,
you are a Shakespearian romance
you yourself are something in which the right
set of eyes will marvel at in dream like wonder

lvii.

The human body fully sheds its skin every 27
days. This means that you have never held these
hands, brushed this cheek, kissed this mouth.
This means that we are strangers again, open to
the possibility of a second first.

lix.

Tell me about the hands that broke you like tree
branches. Tell me about the heart that made you
a home, the barren soul that used your dry bones
like kindling in the middle of winter. Tell me
about the house fire, the ashes which you rose
from. Tell me about your resurrection—but don't
you dare tell me that you are not strong enough
this time, don't you dare tell me that you cannot
rise again,
and again,
and again.

lviii.

The greatest tragedy of the human condition is
that we often favor nurture rather than nature.
We favor the heartbreaks, the dishonesties, the
ghosts that haunt our spines, and forget the fact
that nature never lies.

Nature never asks for permission, it
simply just exists, as it is. A cloud will never
refrain from crying, a mountain will always
stand confident, a tree will grow where it is
planted, and it will grow strong, because nature
never denies itself. Nature never doubts or
withholds, it never plays small, it never submits.

Be more like nature. Do not let your mind
taint the beauty in which your heart has felt.
Rather, stay wild within your love, within your
curiosities. Let your passion run raw like indigo
currents, until you have unapologetically, and
ruthlessly, set yourself free.

lx.

Promise me that you will never allow yourself to
be loved in halves again, that you will fall in love
with someone who makes you question why
you ever thought you weren't whole to begin
with. Promise me that you will rise with this
new Spring, that you will thaw your winter
wounds with summers air and pack the gaps of
your heart with its soil—for what a gift it is to be
new again, what a gift it is to grow.

YOUR BONES
ARE PENS,
— WHEN YOU LIVE —
THEY WRITE
YOUR STORY.

lxi.

Remember what you are made of the next time
you think you are bulletproof. You are
white bone and silken flesh; your heart is made
of gold and glass. Stop trying to make
yourself indestructible—like any soft creature it
is in your nature to break, like any soft
creature it is in your nature to heal.

lxii.

I tried so hard not to turn you into poetry.

lxiii.

Survival takes courage, it takes guts to pick up the pieces of the wreckage and move on, to dust off your limbs and bandage your hurts. Survival is more than burying the damage, it is about befriending it—it is about being thankful for how, at a point in your life, it created graveyards within you. For when you look back, you will finally understand that it is nothing short of incredible, how you managed to emerge like wildflowers, from the cemeteries you held within your soul.

lxiv.

Let your words
shine like Spring,
For those with Winter
in their bones.

lxv.

When I ask you about your first love, I am always
secretly hoping that you will say your own name.
Now wouldn't that be beautiful—to above all else,
have a heart that was proud of itself.

lxvi.

Listen—beautiful things are vanishing each and
every day. The world is becoming a hard place. Its
time to take the love you have within yourself
and spread it around the Earth. Its time to
remind the people you meet that they were once
as soft as the sea, that they were once light too.

Love
needs
REINVENTING.

lxvii.

For years you let yourself believe that you were a prison, a home to all of the intervals of time you wasted being confused, or heartbroken, or unhappy. The truth is, there are things inside of you that the world needs to hear, there are breaks and breakdowns that will mend hearts and patch sores. Do not convince yourself that your suffering was futile, that your scars are simply scars instead of stories. Do not keep your past suspended like an anchor in the back of your throat, for it is time to speak. I promise you – the voice you think is simply just a whisper, is actually made of brazen thunder. It will bellow through the bones of those who need it, it will clap within the veins of a seeking heart, and when you least expect it, someone will thank you for sharing the mausoleum of lessons you boarded up within, and you will finally, finally, understand why you had to bleed.

lxviii.

Please forget that love is often a stick of dynamite, burning at both ends. Forget how people can be fireworks within your soul, just waiting to destruct. You cannot care that love is, at times, tragic. You cannot care that it may flee. All you can do is simply try, with every shattered piece of your patchwork heart, to fight for what you feel—to believe that there is more.

lxix.

When was the last time you truly looked at someone?

I mean truly. When was the last time you saw a woman or a man, and did not glance at them in passing, but looked at them as if you finally understood that they were a trove of triumph and tragedy, that they had loved and lost. Never forget that human beings are more than just the framework of their bodies, that they are the summation of a thousand invisible parts, moments. People come to us brimming with hope, and fear. When we truly connect with that, we turn them from ordinary strangers, into layers of rich history,
just waiting to be discovered.

lxx.

Do not just show me how much you love me with
your mouth, your palms, or the shift of your
bodyweight on to mine. No, show me how much
you love me with your life, show me how much
you love me with your joy.

lxxi.

The beautiful thing about love is that it cannot
be manufactured or destroyed. It is carnal, it is
raw; it cannot be discovered where it does not
exist, it cannot be concealed where it thrives. Use
this to your advantage. If you do not feel it where
you lay, I hope you have the strength to walk away,
but if you do,
my god—
I hope you have the strength to fight.

lxxii.

There is a resounding level of strength that can be found inside when you realize that you were made and loved intentionally, just as you are.

lxxiii.

We died a violent death, you and I. We tip toed
along the foundation of something vast,
something that transcended anything our
mortal parts could ever hold within themselves.
There was passion and promise, but we were too
human, too scared. We set our souls on fire
without an escape plan—all we could do was
burn. So we watched as our memories slowly
dissolved into the forms of other people, we
watched as our hearts painfully learned the
consonants and the vowels of someone elses
name. We ran, straight into the eye of a storm,
and we never came out the same.

lxxiv.

You are never really mortal if you
love and inspire someone deeply.
In that, you will always live on.

lxxv.

"Are you happy?"
"In all honesty? No. But I am curious—I am curious in my sadness, and I am curious in my joy. I am everseeking, everfeeling. I am in awe of the beautiful moments life gives us, and I am in awe of the difficult ones. I am transfixed by grief, by growth. It is all so stunning, so rich, and I will never convince myself that I cannot be somber, cannot be hurt, cannot be overjoyed. I want to feel it all—I don't want to cover it up or numb it. So no, I am not happy. I am open, and I wouldn't have it any other way."

lxxvi.

Please, be good to yourself. Do not spend one more slaughtered night focusing on the fact that bad things exist—that people hurt, and break and fracture under the weight of unsaid words and ruptured hearts. Promise me that you will focus on the beauty—the breathtakingly awe-inspiring moments in life that prove to us that we can overcome, the exquisitely remarkable instances that inspire within us the strength, the courage, to heal.

lxxvii.

Your whole self and nothing less; that is what
you must give them. Gift them everything you
have to offer in your stunning mind, and never
worry that you will be left empty. They will take
and take, they will create masterpieces from
your skin, your bone, your spine, and still you will
always be whole—the fire will always find you.

lxxviii.

When I ask you if you are okay, please promise
me that you will speak words cloaked in hones-
ty—even if your voice shakes and trembles. For if
you aren't, I need you to understand that it is
acceptable. Occasionally sadness grows on trees,
and there will be days where you feel like an
entire forest. I will never reject you for that. I will
be there to remind you that you are more than
just a body, you're a soul, and sometimes that
gets sick. After all, if bones can break, minds can
too. Do not be ashamed. Do not flee, do not hide.
You are not ruined or damaged by this, you are
not unworthy. Dawn is waiting to crack within
the shade of you; the warmth is on its way.
Promise me you will stay to greet it.

lxxix.

When I imagine courage I do not see daredevils
or fast cars. I simply envision a man, loving with
every inch of himself—loving despite the past.

lxxx.

How are you supposed to love the darkest, and most flawed parts of the person your heart chooses, if you won't allow yourself to love your own?

lxxxi.

Happiness turned to me and said—"It is time. It is time to forgive yourself for all of the things you did not become. It is time to exonerate yourself for all of the people you couldn't save, for all of the fragile hearts you fumbled with in the dark of your confusion. It is time, child, to accept that you do not have to be who you were a year ago, that you do not have to want the same things. Above all else, it is time—to believe with reckless abandon that you are worthy of me, for I have been waiting for years."

lxxxii.

We used "I love you" like an apology for all of the things we knew we were doing to wound each other, like a final attempt at keeping the fire from burning out, like two beggars just gripping at each other's limbs.

I love you—despite hurting you.
I love you—despite judging you.
I love you—despite being incapable of loving myself.

It took us years to understand that love was not meant to justify hurt; that love alone was never meant to be used as a means of vindicating the problems we didn't fight to change. In the end, we thought that love would save us from ourselves, but after ages of misuse, the only thing that needed saving was love itself.

lxxxiii.

It is believed that touch comes before sight,
before speech. So when I tell you that you have
touched my heart, I do not mean that you have
moved me with traditional language, I do not
mean that you have caressed me with your warm
gaze. When I say that you have touched my heart,
I simply mean that you have touched it with your
own heart; I simply mean that you have changed
my life.

lxxxiv.

You have a quiet within you that sleeps inside
your bones, that stirs within your heart, but you
rarely notice it. Take a minute to truly think—
when was the last time you were fully present?
In a moment, in a feeling, in a state of mind.
When was the last time you left the excess
behind? The last time you tucked yourself away
from outer stimulation and distraction, from the
sights and the sounds, the confusions that you
tend to noose around your veins until you feel
torn down.

Let it go.

Understand that you are more than just a body
you're a soul, and what's good for the body isn't
always good for the whole because we tend to
lose control in the idea of our presence. We touch
but we don't feel. We speak but we don't connect.
We strive for moments of validity but there's
always a regret, a deeper calling, a thirst within
our cells for silence. Our minds seek a connec-
tion with that quiet, with the awareness that you
are so much bigger than this room, than this
city, than anything around you.

Do you understand? What you are made of? The
very stars combust in the night sky with the
same atoms that make up your mind. The trees
breathe the same air as you do, the very salt of
your skin is the same salt that crashes against
shorelines due to the turning of the moon. Can
you feel that? The nature within you? The one you
forget about when your mind starts to race, when

the tribulations of your days gets the best of your grace and your gratitude. Take a step back. Get out of your head and into your body. Can you feel that? Against the dryness of your bones? It's a stillness that speaks from your soul, that removes you from all the ways you get lost in a maze of detachment.

Stop doing. Stop thinking. Stop anticipating.

And surrender. Surrender yourself to the beating of your heart, to the most carnal representation of the strength and the vitality you hold within yourself. Start here. For every time you feel the thud of its presence against your ribcage, I urge you to think: This is my liveness, pounding within me, at this very moment, in which I will never get back. And every time you allow your mind to take you away from the awareness you find inside remember: Your hands will never feel this again. Your ears will never hear this again. Your cells will never ignite like this again. So connect. Connect with the physicality of your nature. Of your stillness. Of your moment.

They don't teach you how to hurt. How to truly hurt, to truly feel every inch of your body on fire and be at peace with it. To see your grandfather or your brother grieving in front of you, to see your mother throw herself into the plot and beg for the world to take her too. They don't teach you how to hold someone who is delicate and lost, who just needs to feel the sincerity within your cells against their aching skin. They don't teach you how to cry with your best friend, how to compassionately be there for another human being because you were once there as well.

No, they don't teach you how to love. How to truly love, how to selflessly commit to someone else, how to give your heart to another human being and trust that their palms won't crush your gift. They don't teach you how to love yourself, how to build a temple within your ribcage that doesn't wax and wane with validation, that doesn't turn to ruins in the midst of your confusion. They don't teach you how to stand alone, in pure confidence, in ruthless certainty of your matchless heart.

They don't teach you resistance, resilience. They don't teach you how to make ends meet, how to get up each and every solitary day as a single mother or a struggling twenty something when all you want to do is sleep. They don't teach you how to live with your demons, with your disappointments, they don't teach you how to figure out who you used to be before you allowed for your flaws to define you. They don't teach you how to push, how to truly push back at life when it closes in on you, how to remind yourself of white-hot light in the midst of a sapphire dark spell. They don't teach you how to survive.

See, if math were a life lesson we would learn how to count the number of times we've been let down. We would learn to subtract all of our pride, leaving us with understanding, leaving us with a will to persist. If geography were that of existence, we would take fieldtrips to the redwoods and breathe in their beauty, we would learn about how the universe is mapped out within our veins, how the Milky Way and Cassiopeia are dancing within our brains. If art were a life lecture, we would take a magnifying glass to the cracks within our bodies, and we would see just how whole we are in spite of them, just how artistic our own wounds can be, like famed Renaissance mosaics, like chipped one hundred year old paintings.

No, they don't teach you what it takes to be human, what it takes to be real. For the reality of life thrives in our experiences of it. The marrow within our bones is made up of practice; it is made up of the memories that defined us, the moments that surprised us, that hurt us, that challenged us. We are walking, breathing lessons, our cities are our institutes, our peers are our professors, our mistakes are our tutors. Make sure you are constantly educating yourself; make sure you are constantly learning.

When I was growing up I dedicated my heart,
with reckless abandon, to the idea of finding my
soul mate. Wistfully I listened to stories of the
ancient gods, and how they split each and every
single human being into two parts. We were one
part, and the other half, our counterpart, would
make their way into our lives at some point,
completing us and pouring into us a love that we
had never experienced before. Now I am realizing
that such a philosophy is actually more harmful
than it is valuable.

I do believe that we should feel something
unique when we finally meet the person we
choose to spend our lives with, and I do believe
that we should be inspired and deeply moved by
the love we are gifted in life. However, we are not
incomplete human beings, and there is no one in
the world who is going to fill the voids of our soul
other than ourselves. That rush of feeling that we
want to experience when we meet our soul mate
is not a feeling that is bred from the stitching
together of two reunited hearts, and it isn't as
tell tale as we often think it is.

In reality, there is more to forever than simply
finding someone who you feel extremely
connected to. We have to stop allowing this
surge of feeling to act like a compass towards
healthy relationships. Distinctive and enchant-
ing feelings for someone are a great compass,
but they shouldn't be the only thing we take into
account when falling in love. We cant keep
striving for this absolute, perfect love, because

when life throws us some less than perfect situations we are going to need more than connection, more than an emotional upwelling of exhilaration. We are going to need pragmatic love, we are going to need levelheadedness, we are going to need a person who fights for us every single day—who chooses us in spite of circumstances.

Soul mates don't exist. Real human beings do. The goal is to redefine this idea of the perfect kind of love, and turn it into an openness to a very real kind of love. You aren't going to find someone who completes you, and you shouldn't strive for that. Instead, strive to find someone who inspires you to complete yourself. Strive to find someone who pushes you, and breaks into you in ways that allow for you to see all of the potential that exists within your bones. Strive to find someone who your loves grows with—slowly, strongly. Strive to find someone who ignites within you the motivation to love in the most enduring of ways because, luckily, that kind of person does exist.

ACKNOWLEDGEMENTS

To the One:

You inspired within me a love I still do not fully understand. For that, I owe you everything. You dug through the Earth of me, destroying the layers of doubt I grew inside my feeble heart. Thank you for getting your hands dirty, thank you for always being the one to try. You are pure beauty manifested in human form, I will only ever want to give you the world.

To the Nomad:

You promised me love, but you gave me silence. I should have known the first time—that you were a deathwish, but I came crawling back into your arms like a prideful child. Thank you for the distance, for you are a fire burning within me now. You are a blood flame, a crimson blaze. You are the reason I woke up in the middle of the night, seeking a getaway from the pain, and that is when I picked up the pen and finally bled—that is when I found my voice again.

To the Life Source:

Thank you for inspiring me to be strong when I felt weak, for inspiring me to speak when I felt heavy words at the back of my throat. Thank you for telling me that it was okay to be sad when I did not quite understand the grief—that if a bone can break, a mind can too. Thank you for understanding that despite the fact that I laughed with all of the vigor in my body, I held a hurt within me that I had to face. You are the reason I have made it this far, you—you without the guidelines, you without the arms of a mother to hold you like you held me—you. You gave me life not once, but twice.

To:

The New Yorker
The Little Bird
The Music
The Changemaker
The Cabin

About the Publisher:

Thought Catalog Books is a publishing house owned by The Thought & Expression Company, an independent media group based in Brooklyn, NY. Founded in 2010, we are committed to facilitating thought and expression. We exist to help people become better communicators and listeners, to engender a more exciting, attentive, and imaginative world.

We like email: hello@thoughtcatalog.com.

About the Author:

Bianca Sparacino was born in Toronto, Ontario and is an avid writer, artist and scientist.

Visit her online at www.facebook.com/rainbowsalt